CREATIVE SCIENCE FOR YOUNG CHILDREN

by Betty Foster
Annetta Dellinger
Sarah Askins House
Susan Cowles Hudson
Jo Ellen Weems
illustrated by Mina Gow McLean

THE CHILD'S WORLD

ELGIN, ILLINOIS 60121

INTRODUCTION

Creative science—that's a way of saying this book features hands-on projects that let young students experience the joy of learning. Working experiments makes learning science an enjoyable encounter, as it should be.

NOTE TO TEACHERS

It is not the authors' intent to limit any experiment or project to the designated day or season. Though the creators thought these projects could enhance the suggested special days, most of the experiments could be used for any occasion or season.

Scientific materials and specimens may be obtained from the following addresses:

Eastern states contact:

Carolina Biological Supply Company
Main Office and Laboratories
Burlington, North Carolina 27215
(919) 584-0381   Toll-free number: 800-334-5551
NC customers call 800-632-1231

Western states contact:

Carolina Biological Supply Company
Powell Laboratories Division
Gladstone, Oregon 97027
(503) 656-1641   Toll-free number: 800-547-1733
OR customers call collect: (503) 656-1641

Editor: Evelyn Solomon
Contributing Editors: Sandra Ziegler, Janet Riehecky

Library of Congress Cataloging in Publication Data

Creative science for young children.

(Around the year books)
1. Science—Study and teaching (Elementary)
2. Science—Experiments.   I. Foster, Betty, 1920-
II. McLean, Mina Gow.   III. Series.
Q181.C73   1988   372.3'5   87-23893
ISBN 0-89565-415-6

1 2 3 4 5 6 7 8 9 10 11 12 R 96 95 94 93 92 91 90 89 88

CONTENTS

JANUARY/FEBRUARY/MARCH

APRIL/MAY/JUNE

JULY/AUGUST/SEPTEMBER

OCTOBER/NOVEMBER/DECEMBER

JANUARY

FEBRUARY

MARCH

Highlights

- New Year's Day
- Birthday of Martin Luther King, Jr.
- Groundhog Day
- Valentine's Day
- Presidents' Day
- Birthday of Alexander Graham Bell
- St. Patrick's Day

It's Freezing

OCCASION: New Year's Day, January 1
PURPOSE: to observe the effect of freezing temperatures on water
MATERIALS: a jar of water

PROCEDURE: On New Year's Day, or any freezing day, pour some water in a jar and place it outside uncovered. After several hours, bring the jar inside and see what has happened to the water. Leave the jar inside and observe what happens to the water.

Tell the children that warm-blooded living things, such as people, are largely made of water and must be protected in cold weather or they will freeze. Discuss ways living things protect themselves from the cold.

Draw a Bird

OCCASION: winter
PURPOSES: to feed, watch, and identify winter birds
MATERIALS: dried-up doughnuts, peanut butter, birdseed, string, writing paper, drawing paper, crayons or felt markers, a book about birds

PROCEDURE: Smear peanut butter around a doughnut, roll it in birdseed, and hang it outside where the children can see it from a window. As birds come to feed, try to identify them. Keep a list of the different kinds.

Help children enjoy the double meaning to the word "draw." First let them draw (attract) birds to the bird feeder. Then let them draw pictures of favorite birds.

Northern Lights

OCCASION: appearance of northern lights (aurora borealis; southern lights—aurora australis)
PURPOSE: to experiment with colors
MATERIALS: several flashlights, colored cellophane paper, white paper, rubber bands

PROCEDURE: Talk about the northern lights, those magnificent natural displays of moving colored lights that occur around the north and south poles. They can be seen in higher latitudes at night. Their appearances most

often coincide with the equinoxes, with periods of great sunspot activity, or with magnetic storms in the atmosphere.

Explain that northern lights can look like patches of light, streamers, arcs, rays, or curtains hanging in the sky. They are most often green, yellow-green, yellow, or red. Sometimes they are blue or violet. Then experiment with your own colored lights.

Cover flashlights with different colors of cellophane paper. Secure the paper with rubber bands. Darken the room. Shine the flashlights on white paper. See what colors can be made by shining two or more flashlights on the same spot.

A Touch, A Feel

OCCASION: winter
PURPOSE: to explore the sense of touch
MATERIALS: a large grocery bag containing as many different items as there are children in the class; use items such as an Artgum eraser, a piece of sandpaper, an apple, an orange, a smooth stone, a piece of chalk, a pencil, a small notebook, a crayon, a paintbrush, a cotton ball, a piece of sponge

PROCEDURE: Everything has its own look, sound, taste, smell, and feel. Discuss the many differences in things around us. These differences make our lives interesting. Tell the children that today they will discover how things feel by touching them.

Gather the children into a circle on the floor, or have each child come to the front of the class one at a time. Do not let the child see the items you have placed in the bag. Let each person take a turn reaching into the bag to pick one item and name it. After naming it, the child should pull the item out of the bag to see if it was named correctly.

Have each child place the identified object on a table and describe how it felt. Do not put that item back into the bag. After the bag is empty and everyone has had a turn, ask if any items would have felt differently had they been cold, hot, warm, wet, sticky, etc.

Surprise Flower Garden

OCCASION: birthday of Martin Luther King, Jr., January 15
PURPOSES: to honor Martin Luther King, Jr.; to understand how plants grow from bulbs
MATERIALS: a one-pound margarine container or bowl, small stones or glass marbles, water, two or three pre-cooled hyacinth bulbs

PROCEDURE: Summarize this material as you talk about Martin Luther King, Jr. Tell the children that there is a holiday to honor him on the third Monday in January. King's goal was that one day all people would live together in harmony, like flowers of many colors blooming in a garden of peace. We can plant a flower garden to honor and remember him.

Show a flower bulb to the children. Ask the following questions: "Which end will the sprout come from?" (Pointed end.) "Where will the roots begin?" (Fatter end.) "What must the bulbs have to make the roots grow?" (Water.)

Have the children place an inch of small stones or marbles in the bottom of a container. Transparent marbles will enable the children to see the growth of roots more easily. Place the bulbs on this base, pointed ends up, about an inch apart. Carefully fill in more small stones or marbles until the bulbs are half to two-thirds covered. Slowly add cool water until it reaches the bases of the bulbs.

Ask these questions: "Where are bulbs usually planted?" (In the ground.) "What starts growing first?" (The roots.) "Is it light or dark in the soil?" (Dark.) Have a child put the container with the bulbs in a dark cupboard or closet. Look at the bulbs daily to check for roots. Keep the water level constant. In a week to ten days a thick root network should be developed. Water level can then be dropped to a quarter of an inch below the bases of the bulbs.

After a four-inch to five-inch spike forms, ask the children, "What do the bulbs need beside water to sprout?" (Sunshine or light.) Let a child

move the bowl to a sunny windowsill. Put a sign beside the flower garden—"In honor of Martin Luther King, Jr.'s birthday." Water will now need to be added more frequently to keep the level the same. (You may want to use this opportunity to observe and learn about evaporation.)

Watch daily for signs of growth. Sprouts will appear and grow into long leaves. Finally, look for the *surprise* growing up in the center. Ask the children to describe what they see. In a few days, buds will be evident. Soon clusters of star-like flowers will appear! Allow the children to smell the beautiful fragrance.

As the life-cycle progresses, ask, "What will happen when the hyacinth bulbs are through blooming?" (The plants will wilt and die.) When the leaves have wilted, the bulbs should be taken out of the container. Hyacinth bulbs need to be kept cold during their dormant stage. If you wish to use them again next year, store them in brown paper bags, open at the top for ventilation, at 38 to 40 degrees.

Pet Rocks

OCCASION: birthday of Martin Luther King, Jr., January 15
PURPOSES: to observe differences and similarities in rocks; to appreciate the differences and similarities in people too
MATERIALS: rocks, books about rocks

PROCEDURE: The day before the lesson, ask each child to find a rock that will fit in his hand and bring it to school.

In class, have each child get acquainted with his own rock. Note its size, color(s), shape, roughness, smoothness, and any distinctive markings. With the help of a book, older children may wish to identify the types of stone in their rocks.

Let each child name his rock. Have each person introduce and describe his rock to the rest of the class. Then mix up all the rocks and have each child find his own rock again. If you wish, let the pet rocks "visit" each other while the class does its work.

You may also want to compare people and other things to rocks. Each person and each rock has individual characteristics.

Hello, Shadow

OCCASION: Groundhog Day, February 2
PURPOSE: to understand about and experiment with shadows
MATERIALS: large sheets of paper, chalk, a bright light (such as a projector light), white paper, black paper, scissors, a white sheet

PROCEDURE: Discuss Groundhog Day. Some people believe that the groundhog, which is also called a woodchuck, can predict what the weather will be. If the groundhog comes out of his home on February 2 and sees his shadow, then winter will last six more weeks. If the groundhog does not see his shadow, then spring will come soon.

Go outside on a bright, sunny day. Have the children look for the shadows of trees, buildings, clouds, fences, animals, playground equipment, and themselves. Explain that the light from the sun shines on many different things, but it cannot shine through them. When the light is blocked by an object, there is a dark place called a shadow.

Try the following experiments:

1. Have the children make the biggest (longest, smallest, shortest) shadow that they can. Ask, "What makes your shadow move?"

2. Divide the class into small groups. Have each group make a shadow with four arms and legs or six arms and legs.

3. Play "Shadow Tag." Let one child be "It." Have the others move about. "It" should try to step on another person's shadow. When "It" succeeds, that person should become "It."

4. Have the children work in pairs. Let them trace their partners' shadows on large pieces of paper or with chalk on cement.

5. Make silhouettes of the profiles of the children's heads for special valentine gifts for parents. First, set up a bright light so it will reflect profiles on pieces of white paper attached to the chalkboard. Trace the shadows. Tape the white papers to sheets of black paper and cut out the silhouettes from both sheets at once. Then mount the black silhouettes on sheets of white paper and the white silhouettes on sheets of black paper. Do this so the silhouettes are in pairs and look at each other.

Pumpin' Fast and Pumpin' Slow

OCCASION: Valentine's Day, February 14
PURPOSE: to understand the importance and function of the heart
MATERIALS: a model or picture of a human heart, a bucket, a tray, water, red food coloring, meat baster, paper, crayons, stethoscope(s) if available.

PROCEDURE: Show a picture or model as you discuss the heart. The function of this muscle is to pump blood through the arteries and veins to all parts of the body. This muscle moves by itself and never stops working as long as a person is alive. Each time the heart pumps, there is a "thump," called a heartbeat. Food, air (oxygen), and water are carried by the blood. Exercise helps keep our hearts strong and healthy. So do good foods and rest.

Add red food coloring to water in a bucket. Place the bucket on a tray to keep spills in one area. Using a meat baster, draw the red water up into the tube and squeeze it out again. Explain that this is similar to what the human heart does, pulling blood in and then pumping it back out. Let the children work this experiment.

Have the children make fists with their hands. Tell them that their hearts are about the same size as their fists. As people grow, their hearts also grow. Their hearts are located near the middle of their chests.

Divide the children into pairs. Have each child listen to his friend's heartbeat by putting his ear to the partner's chest. Ask, "Can you hear his heart beating? Can you count his heartbeats?" Demonstrate how to take the pulse by feeling the vein at the inside of the wrist or on either side of the Adam's apple. Have the children use two or three fingers (not their thumbs) to feel their own heartbeats at a pulse point.

Next, ask the children to walk around the room or gym. Have them listen to each other's heartbeats again and take their own pulses. Ask if there is any difference in the heart rate from when they were sitting. Now, ask the children to hop up and down for about thirty seconds, then listen and feel their hearts beating again. Ask, "Did the heartbeats get slower or faster? Did your heart beat at the same speed as your partner's?" Explain that the heart beats faster after active exercise because more oxygen and nutrients are needed by the body. Let each child make a graph to record the rate of his heartbeat.

If possible, let the children take turns listening to their hearts beat through a stethoscope. Have them describe the sound.

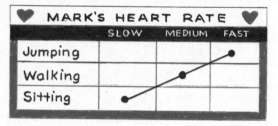

If a medical school is nearby, an intern may be willing to talk to the class about the heart.

Workin' Hard Where E'er They Go

OCCASION: Valentine's Day, February 14

PURPOSES: to understand the basic functions of arteries and veins; to locate several arteries and veins

MATERIALS: cardboard tubes from paper towels or toilet tissue, strong flashlight(s)

PROCEDURE: Working in pairs, have the children listen to one another's hearts, using cardboard tubes pressed to the chest. Discuss the stethoscope a doctor uses for the same purpose. Explain that the sound they hear is the heart pumping blood to all parts of the body. Blood travels through tubes of many sizes called blood vessels.

With the room darkened, help the children locate red lines in their ears and hands by holding the flashlight directly behind these body parts. Explain that the red lines, arteries, carry blood filled with oxygen to all parts of the body. The oxygen is absorbed and used by the body.

Next, in normal light, help the children locate blue lines on their wrists, on the backs of their hands and under their tongues. The lines that look blue are veins. The veins carry blood filled with carbon dioxide from all parts of the body back to the heart. From the heart, the blood is pumped into the lungs where the carbon dioxide is exchanged for oxygen. This fresh blood goes back to the heart and is pumped to the body again through the arteries.

Candy Making

OCCASION: Valentine's Day, February 14
PURPOSE: to demonstrate that substances can be changed when heat is added or taken away
MATERIALS: electric frying pan, water, a heat-proof dish (or a fondue pan with sterno burner), forks, solid chocolate—cut up into small pieces, small twisted pretzels, chunks of apple, slices of banana, waxed paper

PROCEDURE: Show the solid chocolate. Ask, "What will happen to the chocolate if we heat it?" (It will melt and become a liquid.) "Then how could we make it solid again?" (By cooling it.) Tell the children that today they will do an experiment showing that solid chocolate becomes a liquid when heat is added and that it becomes solid again when heat is taken away.

Place the chocolate pieces in a heat-proof dish and set the dish in the frying pan. Pour water in the frying pan to surround the heat-proof dish. Heat the water at a low-medium temperature to melt the chocolate slowly and smoothly. Let the children observe what is happening to the chocolate.

Divide the class into small groups. When the chocolate is melted, have one group at a time use forks to dip pretzels, apple chunks, or banana slices in the chocolate. Put the dipped pieces on waxed paper to cool. Observe that the chocolate is becoming solid again as it is cooling.

While the dipped candy cools, you may wish to make a list of things that are solid at room temperature but become liquid when heat is added, such as crayons, candles, butter, cheeses, and metals. When the candy is dry, have the children wrap it to take home to share with their families for Valentine's Day.

Make a Cloud

OCCASION: a cloudy day
PURPOSE: to discover what makes clouds
MATERIALS: stove or hot plate, kettle or pot of water, plate, mirrors or other panes of glass

PROCEDURE: Have the children observe clouds in the sky. Ask, "What do clouds look like? What color are they? What size are clouds? What funny shapes do you see in the clouds?" Explain that clouds are made of many drops of water coming together. The water drops are so small that we cannot see them by themselves. They are so light that they float in air. The tiny drops of water collect on tiny specks of dust in the air. Clouds look white when the sun is shining on them. The sun lights up all the tiny specks of dust and the water drops in a cloud.

Make a cloud in the classroom. Boil a kettle of water on a hot plate or stove. Have the children observe carefully what happens when the water begins to boil. Ask, "What do you see? What is the cloud made of?" Explain that the cloud of steam coming from the spout is like a cloud in the sky.

Talk about the cloud from a person's breath on a cold day, the cloud rising from a pond, the cloud from a manhole or sidewalk grate, and the cloud from a vaporizer or humidifier. Explain that fog is a cloud close to the ground. Ask the children if any of them have ever been outdoors in a fog.

Ask them to describe the experience—what the fog looked like, how it felt, how it affected sound.

Let each child "collect a cloud" by puffing his breath onto a mirror or pane of glass, such as a window. Help the children understand that their clouds are made up of tiny droplets of water too.

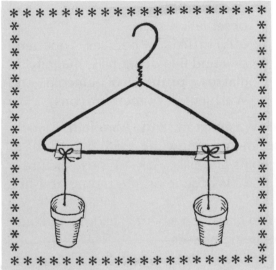

Honest Weight

OCCASION: Presidents' Day, third Monday of February
PURPOSES: to understand the concept of weight; to compare weights of various common objects
MATERIALS: two 6-inch lengths of string, two 8-ounce or 9-ounce paper cups, a wire coat hanger, several small objects such as erasers, paper clips, crayons, pencils, a small rubber ball, etc.

PROCEDURE: Talk with the children about the importance of honesty. Abraham Lincoln was known as "Honest Abe." At one time, Lincoln ran a store, and he probably used scales to weigh things honestly. Scales at supermarkets today enable people to weigh products and be charged honest prices.

To help children grasp the concept of weight, let them help you make a simple balance scale. Tie one end of a string to a paper cup, and then tie the other end to one end of a hanger. Tape the string to prevent sliding. Tie a second cup to the opposite end of the hanger. Tape it also. Hang the scale where everyone can see it and the children can reach it.

Have the children take turns placing small objects in both cups. But first, let them guess which objects they think will be heavier. Allow the children to contribute whatever small items they may have at their seats. Observe and talk about what happens to the scale as items are placed in the cups.

Magnified Presidents

OCCASION: Presidents' Day, third Monday of February

PURPOSES: to learn how to use a magnifying glass for observation; to sharpen visual awareness and observation skills

MATERIALS: pennies, quarters, one and five dollar bills, magnifying glasses, pictures of Lincoln and Washington, paper, crayons

PROCEDURE: Talk about George Washington and Abraham Lincoln —their childhoods, homes, accomplishments. Show the children pictures of the two presidents. Then display the coins and bills. Ask, "Whose picture is on the quarter and one dollar bill?" and "Whose is on the penny and five dollar bill?"

Demonstrate how to use a magnifying glass. Let several children at a time view the bills and coins through magnifying glasses.

Have the children use the magnifying glasses to answer such questions as: What letter is under the date on your penny? How many columns are shown on the Lincoln Memorial? What is on top of the pyramid on a one dollar bill? How many stars are above the eagle on a one dollar bill? What can you see inside the Lincoln Memorial on a new penny? What colors can you see on a bill? On a five dollar bill, can you see the buttonhole in Lincoln's lapel?

Beaver Works

OCCASION: winter thaw

PURPOSE: to show how a dam works

MATERIALS: milk carton, piece of cardboard, flat pan, container of water

PROCEDURE: Talk about beavers and their practices of building houses or lodges in streams or rivers. The lodge entrances and emergency exits are under the water as a protection from enemies. If the water at the chosen site is not deep enough to cover the entrances and to provide an underwater food

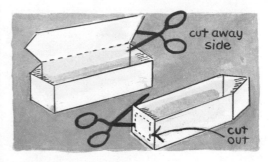

storage place, the beavers build a dam of tree trunks, branches, mud, and stone. The dam slows or stops the flow of water in the stream, and water collects in a pool behind the dam. People also build dams in order to control the flow of water in rivers or streams.

Let the children help prepare the milk carton to show how a dam works. First cut away one side of the milk carton and cut out a square from the carton bottom as shown in the illustration. From the cardboard, cut a rectangular shape to fit inside the end of the milk carton. Place the rectangular piece in the end of the carton, covering the opening.

Place the carton in a flat pan. Have the children pretend that the carton is a stream bed. Pour water in the carton. Raise and lower the piece of cardboard to release water. Pour more water in the carton as needed. Let the children take turns controlling the water flow by raising and lowering the barrier.

Bell's Telephone

OCCASION: birthday of Alexander Graham Bell, March 3
PURPOSE: to demonstrate how sound travels through telephone wires
MATERIALS: two empty tin cans, a 10-foot to 12-foot length of string, masking tape

PROCEDURE: Put tape around the rims of the cans where tops were cut away to make the edges safe. Use a hammer and nail to punch a hole in the bottom of each can. Thread an end of the string through each hole. Tie knots in the ends of the string so that the string will stay connected.

Give a can to each of two children. Have them stretch the string taut. Let one child talk into his can while the other one listens in his. Explain that talking into one can makes the bottom of the can vibrate. The vibrations move along the string and make the other can vibrate. When the listener's ear feels the vibrations, he hears the words spoken.

Leprechaun Magic

OCCASION: St. Patrick's Day, March 17
PURPOSE: to understand how plants absorb water through their veins
MATERIALS: red and blue food coloring, a crisp, inner stalk of celery with leaves, two clear glasses, water, saucer, a sponge, cotton balls, absorbent paper towels

PROCEDURE: First, discuss the lore of leprechauns with the children: the mischievous ways of leprechauns, their pots of gold, how they must tell where they hide their gold if caught, how they disappear, their magic, etc. Then ask the class if they would like to make a snack a leprechaun would enjoy.

Allow the children to color water in two glasses: bright red food coloring in one and bright blue food coloring in the other. Split the celery stalk lengthwise part way up. Also cut a bit off the bottom. Put one half of the stalk in the blue water, the other half in the red. Tell the children they will have to wait to see what happens. (The water will be absorbed into the celery, turning the veins and leaves red or blue.)

During the waiting time, demonstrate absorption. Put a small amount of water in a saucer. Let a child put a sponge in the water. Ask, "Where did

the water go?" (Into the sponge.) Explain that this is called absorption. Let the children take turns demonstrating absorption with the cotton balls, paper towels, and sponge.

In about half an hour, check the celery stalks for the two colors. Have the children observe any lines of color and colored leaves. Continue to watch the celery for a day. Then slice off a piece of the celery. Let the children examine the cut end and discuss what they observe. Lead the children to understand that the celery, a plant, absorbed the colored water, just as it absorbs plain water when it is growing in the ground.

About Sprouts

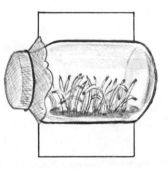

OCCASION: St. Patrick's Day, March 17
PURPOSES: to show absorption; to grow sprouts
MATERIALS: alfalfa seeds, a one-quart to two-quart clear jar with lid, water, cheesecloth, a rubber band

PROCEDURE: Talk about how green the country of Ireland is. Explain that trees, grass, shamrocks, etc., grow in such profusion in Ireland because the climate is very moist. Growing plants absorb water from the ground.

Tell the children that they can grow green sprouts in the classroom. Ask one child to fill the jar with water. Have another child put two tablespoonfuls of alfalfa seeds into the jar of water. Screw on the top. Explain that the little seeds need to soak for a day so that they can absorb water.

The next day, remove the jar lid and cover the mouth of the jar with a square of cheesecloth secured with a rubber band. Drain and rinse the seeds in the jar. Explain that the little seeds did not absorb all the water, but that they absorbed all they needed to begin growing. Before the children go home, rinse the seeds again and lay the jar on its side.

Each day have a child rinse the seeds when class begins in the morning and just before school is out in the afternoon. Drain the water and leave the jar on its side after each rinsing. The jar may be left on a table for the children to observe.

In three or four days the sprouts should be ready for harvesting. Let all the children who wish have a snack of sprouts. Those who bring their lunches may wish to put some sprouts inside their sandwiches. Reinforce the idea that the seeds sprouted because they were able to absorb water as they grew.

Tasty Greens

OCCASION: St. Patrick's Day, March 17
PURPOSE: to explore the sense of taste
MATERIALS: paper cups; a pitcher filled with water, dyed green with food coloring; a pitcher of green lemon-lime drink; a diagram of the taste regions of the tongue; paper plates; a variety of green foods, one taste of each per child. (You may ask the children to bring green foods, such as cucumbers, celery, spinach, broccoli, lettuce, cabbage, limes, zucchini, olives, green peppers, green grapes, green apples, peas, green jelly beans, lime sherbet, green marshmallows, pistachio pudding, sweet pickles, dill pickles, etc.)

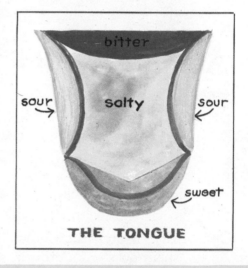

THE TONGUE

PROCEDURE: Give each child a cup half-filled with green water. Ask the children what flavor the drink will have. Ask how they know. After they have tasted the water, ask them if the drink tasted the way they expected. Repeat the procedure using the lemon-lime drink. Discuss how our eyes can fool us, and how we must try foods to know the way they taste.

Then enjoy sampling a smorgasbord of green foods. While the children are eating, explain and locate the tongue's centers of taste: sweet, bitter, salty, and sour. Discuss the taste, texture, and appearance of the green foods. Ask, "Which of the foods are nutritious? Which are not? To what food groups do the nutritious foods belong?"

APRIL

MAY

JUNE

Highlights
- April Fool's Day
- Easter
- Earth Day
- Mother's Day
- World Environment Day
- Father's Day

Fooling with Mirrors

OCCASION: April Fool's Day, April 1

PURPOSE: to understand how a mirror works

MATERIALS: mirror, writing paper, pencils or crayons, a pane of clear glass with smooth edges or a window

PROCEDURE: Show a mirror to the class. Tell the children that a mirror is an "April fooler" because it makes things look backward. Pass the mirror around or have the children take turns looking in a mirror in the classroom. Explain that a mirror is a sheet of glass that has a thin coating of silver on the back. Any light that hits the coat of silver bounces back. This bouncing back is called reflection.

Have the chidren write their names on sheets of paper. Then have them hold their names in front of the mirror. Explain that the names appear to be backward because the light bounces off the sheets of paper to the silvery coat and bounces straight back.

Next, have the children hold their names behind a pane of clear glass. Explain that looking through clear glass is almost like looking through air. The children's names do not look backward because the light goes straight through the glass to the paper.

Let the children discuss mirrors that they have. Talk about ways mirrors are used. For example, they show us how we look. In cars, they make it

possible for the driver to see behind without turning around. They are used for entertainment in fun houses and in telescopes to study space. Doctors and dentists use mirrors to examine parts of the body they couldn't see otherwise.

Try these other mirror activities:

1. Do some mirror doodling. Have each child start in the center of a sheet of paper, with a crayon or pencil in each hand, and draw doodles and squiggles with both hands moving at the same time in opposite directions.

2. Play mirror images. Let the children pair off and stand facing their partners. Have one child of each pair pretend to be the mirror image of the other. The "image" will need to move his body as the other child does, but his poses must reflect rather than be exactly the same.

It Looks Bigger

OCCASION: April Fool's Day, April 1
PURPOSE: to experiment with and understand a magnifying glass
MATERIALS: a magnifying glass, leaf, sponge, piece of cloth, button, other small objects

PROCEDURE: Show the class a magnifying glass. Tell the children that a magnifying glass "fools" our eyes by making things look bigger than they actually are. Explain that the magnifying glass is a piece of glass that is thin on the edges and thick in the middle. Light from the sun or light bulbs hits an object and bounces back through the glass. The magnifying glass bends the light and spreads it. By the time the light comes to your eyes, the object looks bigger than it actually is.

Let the children take turns observing the various objects through a magnifying glass. Discuss ways the magnifying glass is useful. Examples: threading a needle, helping to read fine print, working on small watches, etc.

Eggs-ellent Touch

OCCASION: Easter

PURPOSES: to develop an awareness of the sense of touch; to feel differences in textures

MATERIALS: six or more plastic hosiery eggs, blindfold, materials with a variety of textures (lace, pom-poms, sandpaper, puffy stickers, rickrack, foil), glue for plastics, Easter basket

PROCEDURE: Using glue for plastics, decorate the eggs with materials of various textures and shapes. Make each egg very different for young children; more similar for older children.

At an interest center separate each egg into halves. Set each open end down on a table, mixing up the halves. Have children work in pairs. Let one child put on the blindfold and attempt to find and put together the matching halves through the sense of touch. The child's partner may encourage and guide, as well as place the matched eggs in the basket. Then the partners may exchange places.

Ask questions about the textures of the various materials. Which felt the nicest? Which felt uncomfortable? Which felt rough, smooth, soft, etc.?

Goo and Slippery Slu

OCCASION: a rainy spring day

PURPOSE: to observe and discuss changes that occur in certain materials when water is added

MATERIALS: a dishpan, partially filled with water; various items from the classroom

PROCEDURE: Observe some soil before and after a rain. Ask, "How did the rain make the soil different?" Discuss changes the rain makes in the trees, grass, sidewalks, and other outside things. Compare the differences in ways the various things look, smell, feel, and sound when they are wet or dry.

Find out what happens to other things when they get wet. Dip and soak a sheet of paper, cardboard, pencil, eraser, etc. Observe the changes and feel the textures. Ask which items can be used when wet and which cannot.

Rain Check

OCCASION: April showers or any rainy day

PURPOSE: to chart rainfall

MATERIALS: rain gauge, ruler, chart, felt marker

PROCEDURE: For a specific period of time, a week or a month, collect rain in a rain gauge (see page 26). At about the same time every day, measure the rainfall during the previous twenty-four hours. Enter the amount on a chart. Talk about which days have the most and the least rain. Count the number of rainy days and the number of dry days. See how many there are in a row.

Note: This project may be expanded to include an area's total weather. On the chart include a column for temperature and one for other facts such as windy, cloudy, sunny, etc.

Make a Rain Gauge

OCCASION: spring
PURPOSE: to measure rainfall
MATERIALS: large-mouthed glass jar, thin glass bottle that is same diameter its whole length (an olive bottle, for instance), plastic funnel to fit bottle, ruler, china marker

PROCEDURE: Mark one inch from the bottom on the side of the large-mouthed jar. Add water to that level. Pour the water from the large jar into the thin bottle. Mark where the one-inch of water comes. Divide that one-inch section into four, six, or eight equal parts. Mark these. Then add measurements for another inch or more on your thin bottle. If you are using the metric system in your class, you may prefer to mark the rain gauge in both inches and centimeters. Show the children that one inch equals 2.54 centimeters.

Have the children choose a place to collect rain. Lead the children to understand that the jar will need to be in an open area because if it is obstructed, the rain it collects will not be an accurate reflection of the rainfall. Put the large jar in the selected spot. When the children check the jar and find water in it, let them measure it by pouring it into the homemade rain gauge. Compare each measurement to the previous one.

Magnificent Magnifiers

OCCASION: spring
PURPOSES: to demonstrate that water magnifies objects; to understand the principle of a microscope
MATERIALS: a large plastic pail, plastic wrap, string or a large rubber band, clear water, a microscope, a small comic picture, two pencils, a magnifying glass

PROCEDURE: Cut out two or three fist-sized holes from the side of the pail. Stretch a sheet of plastic wrap loosely across the top of the pail. Secure it around the rim with string or a rubber band. Fill the depression in the loose plastic wrap with clear water.

Tell the children to choose objects that can be held in their hands and will fit through the holes in the pail. Allow the children to take turns holding their chosen objects under the plastic wrap. Have them each observe that looking at an object through the water makes the object appear to be larger. Ask, "What does magnify mean?" (To enlarge, to make bigger.)

Show the class the microscope. Explain that microscopes help us to see things that are too small for us to see with our eyes alone. A microscope uses two or more magnifying glasses or lenses to make objects look bigger. Let the children take turns looking through the microscope at the comic picture.

Next, put two pencils an inch and a half apart on a table. Place the comic picture between the two pencils. Stretch plastic wrap across the pencils. Place a drop or two of water on the plastic over the comic picture. Allow the children to take turns looking at the picture through the water. Ask, "What has happened to part of the picture?" (It looks bigger.) Restate that water is a magnifier.

Explain that you will now use a second magnifier to make a microscope. Show the class how to hold a magnifying glass over the water and look through both of them. The magnifying glass must be moved slowly up and down until the picture can be clearly seen. Have each child take a turn looking through both magnifiers. Finally, let the children take turns looking at objects through the magnifying glass and the water over the plastic pail.

A World of
Rainbow Colors

OCCASION: spring rainbow
PURPOSES: to understand and demonstrate how a rainbow is made; to use
a prism; to mix primary colors
MATERIALS: a picture of a rainbow, clear plastic glasses, water, white
paper, a prism, tempera paints, paintbrushes, several swatches of fabric,
white foam egg carton or ice-cube tray, food coloring

PROCEDURE: Show a picture of a rainbow and talk about how a rainbow
is made. Explain that white light from the sun is made up of the various colors. As sunlight shines through raindrops, the light is bent and separated into
colors. The result is a beautiful rainbow in the sky.

Name the rainbow colors. From the outside of the arc to the inside, the
rainbow's colors are always in the same order: red, orange, yellow, green,
blue, and violet. If you were an airline pilot flying a plane toward a rain storm
with the sun behind you, you might see a circle rainbow. Ask the children to
tell about times they have seen rainbows.

Try the following projects with your class:

1. Go outside on a bright, sunny day. Set a half-full glass of water on a
piece of white paper. Tilt it back and forth. You will see a rainbow on the
paper. Let each child make his own rainbow. Ask, "What colors do you see
in the rainbow?"

2. Show a prism to the class. Hold the prism in a ray of sunlight and turn it
to project the spectrum of colors on the wall or a sheet of white paper. Explain that a prism affects light the same way that water does.

When a prism is used to separate sunlight into its colors, the result is called
a spectrum instead of a rainbow. Ask what colors the children see in the
spectrum. Let each child have a turn making a spectrum with the prism.

3. In an art center, using white paper, tempera paints, and a paintbrush,
demonstrate how to mix colors. First mix yellow and blue together. Ask,
"What color do yellow and blue make?" (Green.) Next mix yellow and red.
"What color do yellow and red make?" (Orange.) Mix red and blue together.
"What color do red and blue make?" (Purple.)

On a second sheet of white paper, make a picture of a rainbow using only

red, yellow, and blue paints. Make a wide red band to be the top of the rainbow. Continue by painting a yellow strip over the bottom half of the red band. Ask, "What happened?" (The color orange was created, which is next in the rainbow.) Paint yellow under orange. Paint blue over the bottom half of the yellow. Continue discussing with the children what colors are being made. Paint blue under the green. Next, paint red over the bottom half of the blue. As you do this, the colors will blend to create a rainbow.

Let each child experiment with mixing colors on one sheet of paper. Have each one paint a rainbow on a second sheet.

4. In the science area pour water into several sections of the egg carton or ice-cube tray. Put fabric swatches nearby. First ask a couple of children to mix coloring in the water of one section to match the color of one of the swatches. Then let others work two or three at a time mixing colors to match swatches. Help the children to explore and understand how to make orange, green, purple, and brown.

 # From All Over the Ground

OCCASION: Earth Day, April 22
PURPOSES: to become aware of soil; to observe and describe some of the physical properties of soil
MATERIALS: various soil samples, newspapers, white paper, spoons, magnifying glass, small clear jars with lids

PROCEDURE: Ask the children to bring in samples of soil in small clear jars. Also provide soil from a park, roadside, and natural locations in your area such as a river bank, beach, desert, etc. Let each child tell where his sample was found: yard, garden, under the grass, trees, bushes, etc.

Spread newspapers on the floor. Give each child two or three sheets of white paper (8½″ × 5½″ or smaller) to put on the newspapers. Spoon separate soil samples onto each sheet for examination and comparison. Have the children look for pieces of leaves, twigs, rocks, sand, etc. Ask them to describe their samples. What colors do they see? How does their soil smell? How does it feel? Let the children take turns viewing their samples through a magnifying glass.

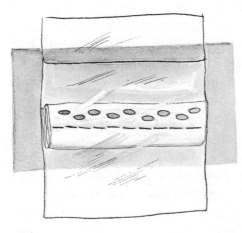

Among the Mung Plants

OCCASION: Earth Day, April 22
PURPOSE: to discover what plants need to grow
MATERIALS: plastic sandwich bags, paper towels, mung bean seeds (available at health food stores), water, refrigerator

PROCEDURE: Ask an aide to help children at an interest center. Have each person fold a paper towel into a one-and-a-half-inch strip. Fold the strip to the width of a plastic sandwich bag. (See illustration.) Insert the folded strip part way into the plastic bag and staple through all the thicknesses of the bag and towel, placing the staples right next to each other in a line across the width of the bag.

Have the children plant 10 to 12 seeds in the pockets of their bags so that the seeds are all on the same side and visible through the plastic.

Discuss what plants need to grow: warmth, light, food, and water. Help the children understand that the food for sprouting is stored inside the seed. The sun will provide light and warmth. The children themselves will provide the water.

To water each bag, dribble one tablespoon of water along the towel. Allow it to soak in. Then add slightly more if necessary. Keep one bag of seeds moist, but store it in the refrigerator. Tape all the other bags of seeds to a wall, poster board, or window, in indirect sunlight. Have the children water all but one of these bags and check them daily to be sure they are keeping the paper towels moist.

Monitor the growth of seeds in all the bags. Compare the differences in the plants in the regular bags, the one in the refrigerator, and the dry bag, and discuss the reasons for the differences.

In a few days, the children will be able to observe the roots develop and grow down into the bags and the stems and leaves sprout up above the bags.

Amazing Changes: Tadpoles

OCCASION: springtime

PURPOSE: to observe the natural wonder of tadpoles changing into frogs

MATERIALS: an aquarium or fish bowl with a screen top; tadpoles, found in a pond or creek or ordered from a supply house (see p. 2); if available, a clump of clear jelly-like frog eggs with black dots in the centers; insects or fish food; pictures of frogs, drawn to actual size

PROCEDURE: Discuss frogs. Ask the following questions: "What can a frog do?" (Swim, jump, croak, and catch insects.) "Where do frogs live?" (On land or in water.) "Where do they lay their eggs?" (In water. Show some, if possible.) "What are the frog's babies called after they hatch?" (Tadpoles or pollywogs.) "How long will it take eggs to hatch into tadpoles?" (4 to 21 days.)

In class, pour pond or creek water containing tadpoles into the fish bowl or aquarium. Make sure there are rocks or something out of the water for the frogs to sit on.

Have the children observe the tadpoles. Ask, "Do they look like baby frogs?"(No, they look more like tiny, dark fish with wiggly tails. They have no legs and their skin is not a greenish color with spots.)

Every day check the tadpoles for any changes. Tadpoles develop into frogs in this order over several weeks: 1. Breathing gills (slits on side of head) close. 2. Hind legs begin to grow. 3. Front legs start to appear. 4. Skin becomes smooth looking and has spots. 5. Tail seems to disappear (it is absorbed).

Feed the tadpoles insects or fish food. Do not leave the aquarium in hot sunlight.

When the tadpoles have become frogs, place a screen top over their container to keep them from jumping out. Talk about and compare sizes of different kinds of frogs. View pictures of them.

Return frogs to their natural home when your study is finished.

Amazing Changes: Chrysalis to Butterfly

OCCASION: springtime

PURPOSE: to observe a chrysalis change into a butterfly

MATERIALS: pictures of monarch butterflies, a chrysalis of a monarch butterfly attached to a twig, a large box with windows cut in the sides and windows and top covered with screen wire (Specific chrysalides may be ordered from Carolina Biological Supply Company. See p. 2. If a hanging chrysalis is collected in the meadow or woods, cut the twig it is on.)

PROCEDURE: Show pictures of monarch butterflies. Discuss the colors of monarchs and other butterflies, what they eat (nectar, a sweet juice down inside flowers), and how they eat (their long, slender tongues reach down into the flowers). Discuss the four stages of a butterfly: egg, larva or caterpillar, pupa in a chrysalis, and butterfly. (*Life Cycle of a Monarch Butterfly,* a sequence chart, is available from The Child's World.)

Show a chrysalis to the children. Place it in the box with some fresh milkweed leaves, and put the box in a shady spot. Explain that the larva or caterpillar formed the chrysalis and is sleeping inside. While it sleeps, its body is changing into its adult form. Keep watching the jar. After a few weeks of waiting, the upper end of the chrysalis will break open. A crushed, velvety mass will come out. At first it will not look like a butterfly. It will cling to the twig with its feet while its wings dry and straighten out. Gradually, it will look more and more like a butterfly. After about a half hour, the butterfly will be able to spread its wings and fly.

When the butterfly has emerged from the chrysalis, the box should be placed by an open window so that the butterfly may fly away and find nectar.

 # Mothers' Helpers

OCCASION: Mother's Day, second Sunday in May
PURPOSE: to understand what machines are and how they help us
MATERIALS: a heavy paper sack, a block or smooth rock, peanuts, salad oil, salt, measuring spoons, a one-cup measuring cup, a bowl, a blender, various machines for display and dismantling

PROCEDURE: Discuss the work mothers do in the home. Make a list of machines that mothers use and discuss how each machine makes a mother's work easier. Ask the children which machines use electricity. Talk about how work was accomplished before the respective machines were invented. Help the children to understand that machines are man-made devices that make work easier.

Compare the hand-grinding process of making peanut butter with the blender method. Here are the ingredients:

1 cup peanuts
4 tbsp. salad oil
½ tsp. salt

When making peanut butter by hand, put the peanuts in a heavy paper sack (or two). Have the children take turns pounding the peanuts into bits with a wooden block or smooth rock. Let the children stir the ground peanuts with the other ingredients in a bowl until thoroughly mixed. Time this.

Make a second batch by putting all the ingredients in a blender and pressing the "blend" button. Turn off the blender and scrape the sides as needed. Note how long it takes the blender to grind and mix the peanut butter.

Try these reinforcement activities:

1. Set up a machine center. Machines that are not normally found in a classroom may be displayed for the children's use: manual typewriter, carpet sweeper, nutcracker, can opener, eggbeater, rolling pin.

2. Have the children help collect discarded machines that can be taken apart such as old radios, clocks, record players, cameras. Be sure that these machines contain no sharp or hazardous parts. Explain that the tools, such as screwdrivers or wrenches, used to take the machines apart are also machines. They are man-made devices that make work easier.

Up, Down, In, Around Air

OCCASION: World Environment Day, June 5
PURPOSE: to demonstrate that air occupies space and exerts pressure

MATERIALS: clear drinking glass, food coloring, dishpan or large bowl, paper napkin, water, lightweight cardboard square slightly larger than the top of the glass, drinking straws, six-ounce juice cans, thin black or brown tempera paint, construction paper, bright tissue paper cut in one-inch squares

PROCEDURE: Fill the bowl or dishpan with water, then color it with food coloring so the experiment can be seen easily. Show the class a glass. Ask the children if there is anything in the glass. Discuss the fact that air takes up space, even though we cannot see it. Air is all around us and fills every open space. Air is in the glass.

Crumple a napkin and put it in the bottom of the glass. Ask the children to predict what will happen when the glass is put upside down in the water. Turn the glass upside down and push it straight down to the bottom of the bowl. Hold it there for a moment, then lift it straight up out of the water. Let the children feel the napkin. Ask, "What kept the napkin dry?" Help the children conclude that water could not get into the glass because the glass was already filled with air that had no place to go. Air kept the napkin dry. Although we can't see the air, we can see its effect. A blanket of air surrounds the earth, and it is important to every living thing. Let the children take turns performing this experiment at the science table.

Next, fill the glass with colored water, and place a piece of cardboard over the glass. Ask the children to predict what will happen if the glass is turned upside down. Holding the cardboard, turn the glass upside down, then let go of the cardboard. Then turn the glass on its side. Ask the children what could be holding the cardboard to the glass. Lead them to conclude that air is pushing from all sides and is holding the cardboard in place. We call the pushing of the air "air pressure." Let the children work this experiment under supervision in the science interest center.

Demonstrate the next project. Fill a juice can with thin tempera paint. Put a straw into the paint, then remove the straw while covering the top with your finger. Explain that air pressure from the bottom keeps the paint

in the straw. Next, release the paint on paper by removing your finger. Explain that air pressure from above pushed the paint out of the straw when your finger was removed. Finally, use the straw to blow the paint in tree-branch designs on the paper. (See illustration.)

While your design is drying, fill juice cans with the thin tempera paint, and let each child perform the experiment for himself. Be sure to caution the class about the dangers of drinking things that might be toxic or harmful, such as paint. When designs are dry, show the children how to crumple a tissue-paper square around a finger tip and dip it in glue. Have them make tissue "flowers" and place them on the tree-branch designs for beautiful pictures of blooming spring trees.

For fun, teach the children this song to the tune of "Frère Jacques."

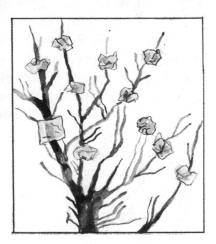

Air fills spaces, and air pushes;
Air is there, everywhere.
Air is what we need; air is what we
    breathe.
Air's all right! Air's out-a-sight!

Jo Ellen Weems

Fathers' Helpers

OCCASION: Father's Day, third Sunday in June
PURPOSE: to observe the work of earthworms and to understand how earthworms help the soil
MATERIALS: a quart to gallon size transparent container, flowerpot shards or gravel, light-colored soil, dark-colored soil, worms, brown sugar, cornmeal, water

PROCEDURE: Ask the children how many of their fathers have gardens and if they ever help their fathers in the garden. What kinds of things do they do to help their fathers and to help the plants in the garden grow?

Then ask this riddle: I'm very small and not too tidy;
I'm very weak, not at all mighty;
I'm very quiet, not a yelper;
But I *am* a gardener's great big helper!
What am I? (An earthworm.)

Talk about how earthworms help the gardener. Packed-down soil makes it hard for seeds to sprout. By eating the dirt for food, earthworms tunnel through soil in gardens and loosen it. This makes it easier for seeds to grow. Earthworms have no backbones, no eyes, ears, noses, or fingers. They are night creatures who like to live in the warm, dark ground. Worms feel with their tails and back out of their holes tail first.

Help the children make and observe a worm ranch. First, obtain a clear container. Place a layer of broken pieces of flowerpots or gravel in the bottom for drainage. Add alternate two-inch thick layers of light-colored and dark-colored soil, ending with light on top. Moisten the soil with water.

Cover the outside of the container with a removable dark paper. When you begin the worm ranch and each week thereafter, feed the worms one teaspoon per worm of a mixture of brown sugar and cornmeal. Check the soil daily to be sure it is moist but not soaked. Worms breathe through their skin. If the soil becomes dry, they will suffocate.

Put in 2 to 12 worms for each quart of the container. The children and their families may supply these from their homes, or they may be bought at a bait shop. Let each child hold a worm gently in his hand to observe the way it moves and feel how it tickles.

Remove the dark paper for a short time each day. Have the children observe where the worms have gone and what their movement has caused to happen to the layers of soil. After two or three weeks return the worm ranch to a garden.

JULY

AUGUST

SEPTEMBER

Highlights
- Independence Day
- Moon Day
- Back to School
- Labor Day
- Johnny Appleseed Day

Bing!
Bang!
Boom!

OCCASION: Independence Day, July 4
PURPOSE: to understand volcanoes
MATERIALS: sand, sandbox or dishpan, a 12-ounce juice can, water, vinegar, dishwashing liquid, baking soda

PROCEDURE: Talk about volcanoes. First, let the children tell about any volcanoes they have seen. Then discuss what sounds they think might be heard when a volcano erupts. In a big explosion, loud rumbles may be heard before a big boom. More often, just rumbling is heard. Sometimes only a hissing of steam is heard.

Explain that most volcanoes build themselves. A crack in the ground leads deep into the earth to a pocket of rock so hot that it is melted. We call the liquid rock *magma*. Some of this may be squeezed up through the crack by the weight of the rock on top of it. More of it may be forced up by steam and other gases formed underground. The force of the gases can even become so great that the top of the volcano can be blown to bits and shoot high into the sky. Not all volcanoes are alike. Some never explode. They just have lava flows. We call magma *lava* when it flows out of the ground.

Let the children help make a pretend volcano. Mix 1 cup of water, ¾ cup vinegar, and ½ cup dishwashing liquid, and set the mixture aside. Place a 12-ounce juice can in a sandbox or dishpan. Let this represent a crack in the earth. Build a mound of sand around the juice can. Pour ¼ cup baking soda into the can. When you want the volcano to "erupt," pour some of the liquid mixture into the juice can. The mixture will bubble upward quickly in the can, but it will make very little noise. Explain that mixing the baking soda with the liquid solution produces gas similar to the gas formed underground that shoots the lava out of a volcano.

A Firefly Collection

OCCASION: Independence Day, July 4
PURPOSE: to learn about and observe fireflies
MATERIALS: a small, clear jar with a perforated lid and a small net (optional) for each child

PROCEDURE: Ahead of time, enlist the help of parents to punch air holes in jar lids. If available, a goldfish net may be used for catching fireflies.

Talk about fireflies. They may be found flitting about on warm spring or early summer evenings just as it begins to get dark. Fireflies are not really flies; they are beetles. Their bodies are about one inch long. They have strong wings that help them fly well. The ends of their tails contain the part that lights up. The light comes on when two special (chemical) substances in the tail mix with oxygen. The male firefly uses his light to attract the female. She shines her light back in answer, although her light is fainter. Fireflies are also called lightning bugs.

Tell the children to catch fireflies with their nets or in their hands, being careful not to squeeze the insects. As each one is captured, it should be placed in a jar with a perforated lid, and the lid should be put back on.

Ask the children to try one or more of the following projects when they have caught several fireflies. Discuss their observations the next day.

1. Observe the fireflies. Find out what part of the firefly lights up. See if the light stays on all the time or if it goes on and off.

2. Take the jar into a dark room or closet and observe it. Do the fireflies make the room any lighter? Do they help a person see any better? Feel the jar from time to time. Does the light from the fireflies make the jar hot?

3. When it's bedtime, take the jar to bed. Put it under the blankets. Watch the lights flash in the dark. Can you see the lights through your blanket? Through your sheet?

Last of all, ask your parent to take the jar outside and let the lightning bugs go free.

Ant Colony

OCCASION: Independence Day, July 4
PURPOSE: to observe that ants, like people, live and work together
MATERIALS: A large glass jar, black paper, cheesecloth, rubber bands, soil, sponge, water, sugar, honey, bread or cracker crumbs, a shallow pan of water (Complete kits are available from Carolina Biological Supply Co. See p. 2.)

PROCEDURE: Talk about Independence Day. Mention that our country was begun by people living and working together in groups called colonies. Today we often celebrate this holiday by going on picnics. Ask if the children have ever been bothered by ants at a picnic. Say that ants live and work together in colonies, and they like picnics. Tell the children that with the following activity they can watch ants at close range, and they can observe how ants work together, which foods they like, and how they carry their foods.

Fill the jar with dirt, leaving a few inches at the top. Cover the outside of the jar with black paper and secure it with rubber bands. Tell your pupils that ants like darkness.

Take the children for a walk outside, and let them look for anthills. Collect several ants and put them inside the prepared jar. Cover the top of the jar with cheesecloth, securing it around the rim with a rubber band. Place the jar in a shallow pan of water to prevent the ants from crawling away. Put the jar in a dark place in the classroom. Keep a small piece of sponge saturated with water inside the jar. Explain that ants need water as we do.

Ants need food too. Let the children feed the ants and watch them eat. Feed them a mixture of honey and water from a bottle cap that you put in the jar. It is also fun to watch ants eat sugar water and bits of bread and cracker crumbs. Ask the children which food the ants like best. How can they tell?

Every two or three days, remove the black paper and cheesecloth, and let the children observe the "ants' new home." Ask them to look for tunnels and little rooms that the ants may have built. Also watch for ants crawling in lines and any other evidence of ants working together.

Who's Afraid of Thunder?

OCCASION: summer storms
PURPOSES: to simulate thunder; to realize that thunder will not harm
MATERIALS: paper bags

PROCEDURE: Wiggle, shake, and strike a paper bag. Have the children listen to the rustling, crackling sound of the paper. Blow up the bag and hold the top tightly closed so that air does not escape. Listen to the loud pop as you hit the paper bag and it breaks.

Explain that the loud pop is caused by the air rushing back together. It is a different sound than that caused by striking the paper. Lightning forces air apart. As the air rushes back together, the sound it makes is called thunder.

Allow the children to perform the experiment.

Classroom

Rocket

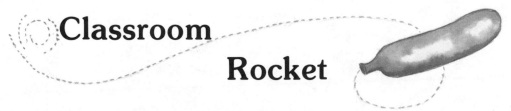

OCCASION: Moon Day, July 20
PURPOSE: to demonstrate how rockets work
MATERIALS: toy oblong balloons, pictures of people in space, kite string, a four-inch to five-inch length of drinking straw, masking tape

PROCEDURE: Ahead of time, ask the children to bring in pictures of spaceships and people in space (or obtain these from NASA, Audio Visual Branch, Public Information Division, Code LFD-10, National Aeronautics and Space Administration, 400 Maryland Avenue, S.W., Washington, D.C. 20546).

Talk about the mission of Apollo 11, the first manned landing on the moon in 1969. Mention that Neil Armstrong and Edwin Aldrin, Jr., landed on the moon in the lunar module, *Eagle*, while Michael Collins orbited in the spaceship, *Columbia*. With older children, discuss the power that was needed to thrust the spaceship into space. Also discuss how *Eagle* was launched from the spaceship, how *Eagle* turned around so its rockets could slow it down as it made its moon landing, and how the rockets were used again to return to *Columbia*.

Blow up a balloon. Explain that the air in the balloon is like the hot gases from a jet or rocket that push a spaceship or rocket forward. Let the neck of the balloon go so that it "rockets" around the room. Have the children observe how the air pushes the balloon.

For a more controlled demonstration, thread kite string through a straw. Stretch the string tautly across the room and secure both ends. One end may be lower than the other. Blow up an oblong balloon, and ask a child to hold the neck tightly closed. Tape the balloon to the drinking straw and slide the straw to the lower end of the string with the neck of the balloon toward the lower end, keeping the balloon tightly closed. Release the neck of the balloon. Observe how the air in the balloon pushes the balloon and straw along the length of the string.

In the science area let the children take turns repeating the demonstration.

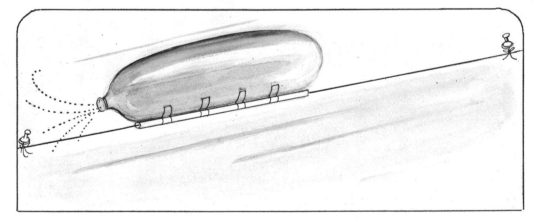

Earth Rocks

OCCASION: Moon Day, July 20
PURPOSES: to learn about moon rocks; to collect and examine earth rocks
MATERIALS: a magnifying glass, a book on rocks, and an egg carton for each child

PROCEDURE: Tell the children that the oldest rocks man has ever found were discovered on the moon! Moon rocks are dark grey and are more than four-and-a-half billion years old. In 1969 two American astronauts, Neil Armstrong and Edwin Aldrin, Jr., were able to walk on the moon. They picked up some of the moon rocks and brought them back to earth. Studying these rocks has helped scientists learn more about the moon.

Have the children pretend they are astronauts, perhaps from another planet. Ask them to collect rocks wherever they go. Have each child arrange his rocks in an egg carton. They may be arranged according to size or color. Let the children examine their rocks with a magnifying glass. Have them look for specks, veins, holes, layers, cracks, flakes, sparkles, and imprints.

First You See It, Then You Don't

OCCASION: summertime
PURPOSE: to demonstrate evaporation
MATERIALS: chalkboard, wet sponge, plate, water, two jars, one lid, felt marker

PROCEDURE: Have a child wash the chalkboard with a wet sponge. Instruct the children to watch the wet board for a few minutes. Ask, "Where did the water go?" Talk about evaporation. Explain that as the chalkboard was drying, the water was turning into drops so tiny that they couldn't be seen and so light that they floated upwards in the air.

Let a child put a few drops of water on a plate and put it in a warm, sunny place. Observe the plate a few hours later. Ask, "What happened to the water?"

One morning mark the outline of a puddle with chalk. Then mark it at different intervals during the day. Ask the children, "What makes the puddle get smaller?"

Place two jars of water on the windowsill. Cover one with a tight-fitting lid. Leave the other uncovered. Mark the water level on each jar every day for a week. At the end of the week observe the difference between the water levels in the two jars. Discuss what happened to the water in the lidless jar. Explain that the water didn't evaporate from the closed jar because it couldn't get through the lid. This explains why Mom puts a lid on the pan when she is cooking food with water. The lid prevents the water from escaping into the air.

The Drier
the Better

OCCASION: summer breezes
PURPOSE: to show that warm air speeds up evaporation
MATERIALS: clothesline (rope, ribbon, or twine), clip clothespins, strong paper towels or handkerchiefs, hair dryer, water

PROCEDURE: Talk about the wind. Define wind as moving air. Explain that you can feel wind blowing by you. On a warm day the wind makes you feel cooler because it blows away water that is evaporating on your skin.

Do this demonstration: Plug in a hair dryer, and set it on cool. Wipe a child's hand with a damp cloth. Aim the hair dryer at the child's hand and turn the dryer on. Ask, "How does the moving air make your hand feel?" (Cool. The moving air carries away the water drying on your skin. The water is drying up because it is taking in heat from your body and changing to tiny droplets of water too small to see. Then the droplets are floating away in the moving air.)

Attach a clothesline to two chairs about three feet apart. Pin wet handkerchiefs or paper towels to the line. Turn the hair dryer to warm and aim it at the hanging items. Turn it on. Let the children observe what happens. Ask, "What will happen to the water?" (It will evaporate into the air.) "On which kind of day will clothes dry more quickly out of doors—on a windy day or a calm day?" (A windy day.) "Why?" (The wind will help carry the evaporating water away faster.) "Will clothes dry faster in a cold wind or a warm wind?" (A warm wind.) "Why?" (Heat increases the speed at which the water breaks up into tiny droplets and floats away.)

Summer Sun

OCCASION: summertime
PURPOSES: to show that sunlight fades colors; to show that sunlight is blocked by opaque objects
MATERIALS: dark blue construction paper, tape, opaque objects such as scissors, jar lids, erasers, cardboard shapes.

PROCEDURE: On a bright, sunny day, put dark blue paper in the bright sunshine. Have the children place opaque objects on the paper. Tape them down if necessary. Leave the items in the sunlight for several hours.

Ask the children: "Does your mother ever close the curtains where the sun shines into your house? Why do you think she does?" Explain that sunlight fades colors. When it shines into houses, it can fade carpets, coverings on furniture, or any colored objects.

When several hours have passed, return to the dark blue paper. Remove the objects. Let the children examine the paper. Have them observe where the sunlight faded the color and where the sunlight was obstructed. Ask, "What outlines can you see on the paper? What made the color fade?" (The sunlight.) "Why did the paper *not* fade where objects were placed?" (The light could not go through the objects.) Explain that if sunlight cannot go through an object, that object is opaque.

Clean Water

OCCASION: National Water Quality Month, August
PURPOSE: to show that water is naturally cleaned by flowing through sand and gravel
MATERIALS: milk carton, clean sand and gravel, pitcher, muddy water, bowl

PROCEDURE: Punch several holes in the bottom of a milk carton. Place a three-inch layer of gravel in the bottom of the milk carton. Place a three-inch layer of sand on top of the gravel. Pour muddy water into the the carton and collect the water in a bowl as it leaks through. Discuss with the class the dangers of dirty water and how nature provides filters for cleaning water.

Seeds Travel Too!

OCCASION: summertime vacations
PURPOSE: to observe seeds and to become aware of how seeds travel
MATERIALS: maple seeds, cocklebur seeds, fruit seeds, dandelion seeds, cattail seeds, etc.; a pair of old socks for each child; magnifying glass

PROCEDURE: Begin the discussion by talking about how people travel. (By car, plane, bus, bike, ricksha, roller skates, on foot, etc.) Tell the children that if seeds could only fall directly to the ground, many species of plants would not survive. Therefore, many seeds have adapted ways to travel. Ask the children how they think seeds travel.

Display various seeds and discuss how they travel. Maple seeds have "wings" that allow them to "fly." Cocklebur seeds attach themselves to the fur of animals and to people's clothes. Seeds for fruit trees are carried by animals that eat the fruit. Dandelion "parachutes" are carried by the wind. Bean seeds are ejected from exploding pods. Cattail seeds travel on water.

For fun, take a seed walk. Before your walk ask the children to bring pairs of old socks to school. Have the children put the old socks on over their shoes. (It doesn't matter if the socks have holes in them.) Take a walk in a meadow and/or forest on a dry day. When you return, take off the socks and see what seeds have stuck to them. Discuss ways in which the different seeds travel, and add them to the display. Place a magnifying glass at the display, and let the children examine the various seeds.

Chunky Chalk

OCCASION: back to school
PURPOSES: to show physical changes in materials; to experiment with color mixtures
MATERIALS: powdered tempera paint, plaster of paris, water, small paper cups, plastic spoons, measuring spoons, paint smocks

PROCEDURE: Have each child measure three tablespoons of plaster of paris and two tablespoons of powdered tempera (these may be one color or mixed colors) into his paper cup. Add three tablespoons of water to each one, and mix well with a plastic spoon. Let harden.

After the mixture has hardened, peel away the cup. Examine the chalk. Talk about the changes in the materials from powder, to liquid, to solid. Talk about what colors were mixed to get other colors. Try drawing with the hardened mixture on paper, cardboard, or the sidewalk.

Working Wheels

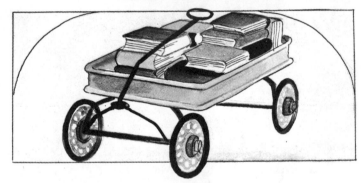

OCCASION: Labor Day, first Monday in September
PURPOSE: to demonstrate that wheels help people move heavy loads faster and easier
MATERIALS: a small wagon, a box similar in size to the wagon, heavy books or bricks

PROCEDURE: Talk about Labor Day. Explain that it is a day set aside to honor people who work. These are the people who have made our country strong and great. Tell the children that over the years many machines have been invented to make work easier. One of the first labor-savers was the wheel. It helps us move things more quickly and easily.

Have the children help load the wagon and the box with an equal number of books or bricks. Tell the class that you need to move all the things to the other side of the room.

Let the children take turns pushing the box and pushing the wagon. (Remind them not to pull the wagon.) Ask them which load was easier to push. Ask why the wagon was easier to push. (It was on wheels.)

Ask the children to name other vehicles that use wheels. Have them watch for ways wheels are used at home, at school, and at play.

Wind Watch

OCCASION: September 15, world's largest weather vane completed at White Lake, Montague, Michigan in 1984: forty-eight feet high, with a twenty-six foot wind arrow

PURPOSE: to discover where the wind blows

MATERIALS: postcards, stamps, zipper-lock plastic bags, helium-filled balloons, world map, journal

PROCEDURE: On several different days, go outside or look out a window to discover which direction the wind is blowing. Tell the children that wind is nothing more than moving air. Observe flags, trees, debris, and other things blowing in the wind.

Print your school's name and address, including U.S.A., on postcards and put stamps on them. Put a note on the back of each postcard asking whoever finds it to print their name, address, and when and where the balloon was found, on the card and mail it. Put the postcards in plastic

bags and attach one to each helium-filled balloon. Let each child release a balloon on a windy day.

While waiting for cards to come back (allow two to three months for responses), help the children understand that not all the cards will be returned. Discuss various things that could happen to the balloons, i.e., get caught in trees or high wires, land in isolated areas, etc.

Hang a world map on the wall. Mark your location on the map. As the postcards are received, mark locations where balloons were found. Keep a journal. Write thank-you letters to the people who return the cards.

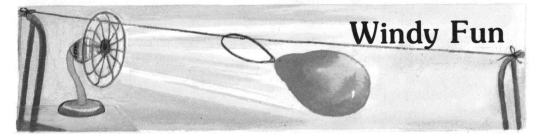

Windy Fun

OCCASION: autumn winds
PURPOSE: to demonstrate that wind is forceful
MATERIALS: crepe-paper streamers, electric fan, balloon, string
PROCEDURE: Ask the following riddle:

> What do you feel, but cannot see?
> What blows your kite into the tree?
> What dries the clothes in the breeze?
> What sails the boat on deep blue seas?
> (Answer: the wind)

Susan Cowles Hudson

Explain to the children that wind is made when air close to the ground is warmed by the sun. The warm air swells (expands), becomes lighter, and begins to rise. Cooler, heavier air moves in under the warm air to fill the space being left by the rising warm air. As the cool air fills the space, it pushes the warm air upward. Meanwhile, the sun is warming the cool air which swells, becomes lighter, and begins to rise making more space for heavy cool air to move in underneath. The moving air is called wind.

Go outside or look out a window on a windy day. Observe objects blowing in the wind. See how far they blow. Talk about ways wind can be helpful (drying mud and clothes; holding up kites, gliders, parachutes, and birds; moving sailboats; etc.).

For fun, do a wind dance outside. Divide the children into two groups and give each child a crepe-paper streamer. Have each group form a line, side-by-side, facing the other group. Call instructions to each group in turn, while the other group watches the swirling, twirling streamers. Suggested instructions: Hold up your streamers and take four side steps to the left, then to the right. Step quickly backward, then forward. Circle the streamers above your heads. Make figure eights in front of you. Turn yourselves round and round, and let the wind blow your streamers.

In the classroom, blow up a balloon and tie the end closed. Tie a four-inch piece of string around the end to make a loop. Hang the balloon by the loop across a length of string tied between two chairs. Have the children take turns blowing on the balloon. See how far each child can make the balloon move in three breaths. Turn on an electric fan to blow the balloon. Ask, "Which wind is stronger? Which wind can blow the balloon farther?"

A Magic Apple?

OCCASION: Johnny Appleseed Day, September 26
PURPOSE: to watch and understand oxidation of an apple
MATERIALS: an apple, lemon juice, two small plates

PROCEDURE: Core an apple and cut it into four sections. Dip two sections in lemon juice and place them on a plate. Place the other two sections on another plate. Ask, "What will happen to the apple sections on each of the plates?"

Observe that the apple sections coated with lemon juice will remain white while the other sections will begin to turn brown within a few minutes. Explain that oxygen in the air combines with the apple to turn it brown. The lemon juice coats the other apple slices with a substance called citric acid. This substance prevents the air from touching the apple, so these sections remain white.

OCTOBER

NOVEMBER

DECEMBER

Highlights
- Child-Health Day
- Columbus Day
- Halloween
- Veterans Day
- Thanksgiving Day
- Christmas
- New Year's Eve

Dust-Debris Collector

OCCASION: Child Health Day, first Monday of October
PURPOSES: to show that air carries many particles of dust and debris; to show that dust and debris will stick to petroleum jelly; to understand that we need to keep our air clean
MATERIALS: a high-intensity lamp such as a projector light, heavy white paper, petroleum jelly, tape, microscope and microscope slides (optional)

PROCEDURE: Discuss what the air is like where you live. Talk about air pollution and the human activities that cause it. Tell the children that although air may look clean, it is filled with tiny pieces of dust.

Darken the room and turn on a high-intensity lamp. Have the children observe the dust particles in the light's beam. Ask them if the air in the room is pure. (No.) Ask if the air is polluted. (Probably not. Dust particles are normal.) Mention that clean air is everyone's concern because everyone must breathe to live.

Give the children sheets of heavy white paper and have them write their names on the backs. Next have them smear a thin film of petroleum jelly on the fronts of the papers. Place the papers in different areas in the classroom and outside. Keep the papers flat by taping them down.

A day or two later, have the children check their papers for dirt particles. Find out which papers have the most dirt particles and which have the least. Ask why some are cleaner than others.

If you teach older children, this activity can be done using the microscope and glass slides. Have each child smear petroleum jelly on a slide and view it immediately through a microscope. Allow them to view their slides a day and two days later to see what particles have accumulated.

Colds and Germs

OCCASION: Child Health Day, first Monday of October
PURPOSE: to understand how germs are spread through coughs and sneezes

MATERIALS: atomizer bottle filled with water, food coloring, newspapers, construction paper or paper plates, scissors, crayons, facial tissue

PROCEDURE: Discuss colds and how your body is affected when you have a cold (coughing, sneezing, sore throat, runny nose, teary eyes, etc.). Explain that you can catch other people's colds and sicknesses from their germs. Ask the children to name the tiniest things they've ever seen. Then explain that germs are even tinier. They are so tiny that they can't be seen except through a microscope. Even though we can't see them, germs are on almost everything. Germs get into our bodies through our noses, mouths, or cuts in the skin. We can help keep germs from getting inside our bodies by keeping ourselves clean and by keeping our hands and things out of our mouths.

Fill an atomizer bottle with water, deeply colored with food coloring. Cover an area on the floor with newspapers. Allow the children to say, "Ahh-choo!" as they take turns spraying the bottle. They will see and feel the tiny droplets fly through the air and see the tiny dots made as the droplets land on the newspaper. Explain that germs fly through the air in a similar way when we cough or sneeze, so we should always cover our mouths.

To reinforce the learning, have the children draw around one of their hands on construction paper. Cut the hands out. Then ask the children to make drawings of their faces on construction paper or paper plates. Ask what a person's mouth and eyes look like when the person is sneezing (eyes closed, mouths open).

Have children wad tissues and glue them over the mouths on their drawings. Then glue on the hands as if they are holding the tissues. Complete the pictures by writing, "Cover your sneeze, please!" at the top of each.

Just for fun, teach this rhyme:

Please share this, and please share that,
Share your treats, and share your toys,
Share your balls, and share your bats,
They're always telling girls and boys.
BUT . . .
When you cough or when you sneeze,
Your germs fly through the air,
So please be sure to cover your mouth.
Germs are not a thing to share!

Jo Ellen Weems

Colored Leaves

OCCASION: fall
PURPOSE: to understand why leaves change colors
MATERIALS: paper sacks, waxed paper, heavy brown paper, an iron, construction paper, glue, crayons or markers

PROCEDURE: Discuss how the leaves of some trees and bushes change color and drop off in the fall. Leaves contain coloring matter called pigment. Pigment can be green, red, orange, yellow, and brown. Normally, leaves contain more green pigment than any other color, causing the leaves to look green. When fall comes, sap in some trees and bushes stops flowing to the leaves. Without sap, the green pigment breaks down because it is unstable. Then the remaining pigments are displayed. We see the beautiful colors. When all the remaining pigments dry up, the leaves fall.

Take the children on a leaf hunt around the school. Collect fallen leaves in paper sacks. Observe all the different colors and shapes of the leaves. In the

classroom, make a big leaf pile. Have the children categorize the leaves by colors and shapes. Find out which color leaves were found most often.

To preserve favorite leaves, iron them between two sheets of waxed paper. To protect the iron, put waxed paper between two sheets of heavy brown paper. Preserved leaves may be used for placemats.

Let the children make leaf people by gluing favorite leaves on construction paper. Using the leaf as a body, have the children add a face, arms, hands, legs, and feet.

Magnets Are Marvelous

OCCASION: Columbus Day, October 12 (landed in New World, 1492)
PURPOSE: to demonstrate magnetic force
MATERIALS: a compass, one or more magnets, small magnetic and non-magnetic objects, a sheet of stiff cardboard and/or thin wood, a glass jar, water, salt

PROCEDURE: Talk about the voyage of Columbus and about how a compass helps a ship find its way at sea. Show a compass. As the children discover how a compass works, explain that magnetism is a force. You cannot see magnetism, but you can see what it does. The earth is a giant magnet that pulls the magnetic arrow on the compass to point north. A magnet will pull some objects but will not pull others. Objects that can be pulled by a magnet are called magnetic.

Allow the children to take turns doing the following experiments. Discuss what the children are seeing and observing. You will want to gear this to the understanding level of your pupils.

1. Experiment to discover which objects can be pulled by a magnet and which cannot. (Most magnetic objects contain iron or steel.)

2. Try pulling a small object with a sheet of cardboard or wood between the object and the magnet. (These are not barriers to magnetic force. This is the reason magnets can hold papers to a refrigerator.)

3. Put a magnetic object inside an empty glass jar. Slide the magnet along the outside. Does the magnet pull the object? (Glass is not a barrier to magnetism.)

4. Pour some water into the jar. What effect does the water have on magnetism? (None.) Add salt to the water. What effect does the salt water have? (None. That is why magnetic compasses can work while a ship is crossing an ocean.)

5. Discuss other uses of a compass, such as while hiking, biking, cross-country skiing, dogsled racing, and deep-sea diving.

Honey, You're the Sweetest

OCCASION: Sweetest Day, third Saturday of October

PURPOSE: to learn about honey, honeycombs, and honeybees

MATERIALS: several blindfolds, a honeycomb or liquid honey, a spoon for each child, pictures of honeybees, a dried-up honeycomb, products made from beeswax

PROCEDURE: Ask for several volunteers to taste something. Blindfold the volunteers. Put some honey or honeycomb on a separate spoon for each volunteer. Have the children taste the honey and describe what they have tasted. Then remove the blindfolds, and let the children see the honey.

Show pictures of honeybees. Tell the children that bees are the only insects that produce food eaten by people. There are about 20,000 species of bees, but only the honeybees make honey. They make it by mixing enzymes from their bodies with nectar from flowers. The flavor and color of the honey depends on the kind of flower from which the nectar is taken. Allow the rest of the children to taste the honey.

Have the children observe the honey in the honeycomb. Explain that honeybees live and work together in colonies. The bees live in a nest called a hive. Inside, they build a honeycomb. It is made of six-sided wax cells. The bees store their honey inside the wax cells. Let the children examine a dried-up honeycomb. Beeswax is used in candles, polishes, plasters, ointments, and lipstick. Display these items if possible.

Scary Skeletons

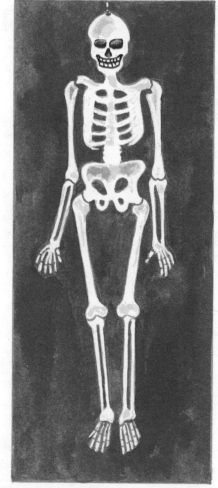

OCCASION: Halloween, October 31
PURPOSE: to understand the purpose of bones in our bodies
MATERIALS: rag doll, Halloween skeleton or a life-sized model of a skeleton, paper, crayons

PROCEDURE: Show the children a rag doll. Explain that without bones we would be as floppy as the rag doll. Our skeletons hold us together like beams hold up a tall building. Our skeletons give us shape and protect us from injury. We have more than two hundred bones in our bodies.

Show the Halloween skeleton. Have the children count the bones that are in one leg. Which bone is biggest? Ask the children to feel their leg bones.

Explain that where bones meet, we have joints. Bones do not bend, so joints help us move. Have the children find joints.

Have the children work in pairs. Let them trace their shapes on large sheets of paper. Have them draw their bones in their shapes. Hang the "Scary Skeletons" in the hall.

Try these other "bony" projects:

1. Have the children bring a collection of bones to class. Talk about how bones feel.

2. Take a trip to a hospital X-ray department, and let the children see X-rays of bones and how X-rays are made.

3. Have an X-ray technician visit the classroom and show X-rays. Perhaps he could also talk about how to keep bones healthy.

4. With older children, identify the bones in the body. Have them memorize the names of the major ones: sternum, ribs, humerus, ulna, femur, tibia, fibula, etc.

One, Two, Three, and Out!

OCCASION: Halloween, October 31
PURPOSE: to learn that fire needs air to burn
MATERIALS: pumpkin, candle, candle holder, matches, clear jar, sharp knife

PROCEDURE: Tell the children that many people put candles in Halloween pumpkins to glow through the jack-o'-lantern faces.

Place a candle in a candle holder and light it. Cover the candle with a clear glass jar so that no air can enter the container. Observe what happens. Explain that the flame uses up all the air inside the container. When all the air is gone, the flame goes out. It must have air to continue burning.

Next, cut out the top of a pumpkin and remove the seeds and strings. Place a candle inside the pumpkin. Light the candle, and on the count of three, put the lid on the pumpkin. Count to three again. If the pumpkin is large, count *slowly*. Take the lid off and see what has happened. Ask the children why the flame went out. Relight the candle and allow the children to take turns trying this.

Finally, cut eyes, nose, and mouth in the pumpkin. Light the candle again, and replace the lid. Count to three, and see what happens. Observe that the candle stays lit because the fire is receiving air through the facial cutouts.

Dry Ducks

OCCASION: fall weather and seasonal changes
PURPOSE: to demonstrate how ducks stay dry
MATERIALS: scraps of brown-bag paper about 4″ × 6″, ½ teaspoon or less of corn or vegetable oil for each scrap, water, sink or dishpan, a duck or bird feather (optional)

PROCEDURE: As cooler days approach discuss the changes in weather. Ask the children how they dress differently for cold weather. Have the boys and girls imagine that they are ducks on a cold fall day. Have them imagine that they are swimming and ducking under the water for food. Pretend a cold north wind has started to blow. Ask the "ducks" how they will stay warm. Will their feathers get wet and freeze?

Explain to the children that a duck has oil glands on its back, where the tail begins. It uses its beak to spread the oil onto its feathers. This is called preening. Preening helps keep a duck's feathers dry, and keeping dry helps keep it warm as well.

In small groups have the children gather around the sink as an aide pours vegetable oil on a scrap of brown paper. Let them observe that the paper absorbs the oil. Then let water run gently over the treated paper. Observe that the water beads and runs off the paper because oil and water do not mix. That is just what happens to a duck's feathers after it has spread oil from its glands onto its feathers. The water runs off and does not soak through to get the duck wet.

If you have a feather from a real duck or bird, let the children take turns dropping water on it to see if the feather does or does not have enough oil on it to shed water.

Shoot a Parachute

OCCASION: Veterans Day, November 11

PURPOSES: to understand how a parachute works; to demonstrate air pressure

MATERIALS: pictures of parachutes; a man's handkerchief or a 15-inch square of fabric, four 15-inch lengths of string or yarn, a wooden spool or a small action figure for each child

PROCEDURE: Discuss Veterans Day, a holiday in honor of men and women who have served their country in the armed services. Mention that many service people must learn how to use parachutes.

Show pictures of parachutes and talk about the purpose of a parachute. Explain how a sky diver wears a parachute. Discuss how the parachute acts as a brake. As the air builds up under the parachute, it pushes upward on the material and keeps the jumper from falling too fast. The pressing of the air against the material is called air pressure.

Have each child make a parachute. Tie a string to each corner of a hand-kerchief or fabric square. Tie the opposite ends of the strings to the spool or action figure. Wrap the parachute around the spool or action figure.

Take the children outside, and let them "shoot" (throw) their parachutes high into the air. Have them watch the effects of the air as the parachutes float down. Reiterate that even though we can't see the air, we can see that it presses upward against the material. The air pressure slows down the fall of the spools or action figures.

If your school has a parachute that is used for physical education activities, the children would enjoy playing games with it.

Why Airplanes Stay Up

OCCASION: December 17, first airplane flight at Kitty Hawk, North Carolina, by Wilbur and Orville Wright in 1903

PURPOSE: to demonstrate the job of the wings in keeping an airplane up in the air

MATERIALS: pictures of airplanes, 1″ × 10″ strips of paper

PROCEDURE: Ask the children if they have ever flown in an airplane. Find out how many have been to an airport. Talk about the parts of the airplane that they have noticed. Show a picture of an airplane. Talk about the shape of the wing. Discuss how it is curved on top and flat underneath.

Explain that the wing's job is to lift the airplane and keep it up. Point out that the wing has a top and bottom. Air under the wing pushes up, and air on top pushes down. If the air under the wing pushes up with more force than the air on top of the wing pushes down, the plane will rise and stay in the air.

With a 1″ × 10″ strip of paper, demonstrate how to make the air under the wing push up with more force. As you pull the paper forward, the pressure of the air pushes straight back and picks up the paper. As you move it faster through the air, more air pressure builds up under the paper. The paper rises because the air pressure under the paper is greater than the air pressure above the paper. On an airplane, the air under the wing pushes up with more force as the propeller pulls the wing through the air faster and faster. As long as the forward speed is maintained, the airplane will stay up because the air pressing upward under the wings is greater than the air pressing downward.

Give paper strips to the children and have them pull them through the air. Observe how the air pressure lifts the paper. Let the children run with the paper strips. Reemphasize that the faster they pull the paper through the air, the more air pressure builds under the paper, keeping the paper up.

Pop Goes the Popcorn

OCCASION: Thanksgiving
PURPOSE: to demonstrate how popcorn pops
MATERIALS: popcorn kernels, electric popper, hotplate or stove, pot with lid, water

PROCEDURE: Talk about the first Thanksgiving, mentioning that the Indians introduced the settlers to corn. Then talk about a special kind of corn—popcorn—as you do the experiment outlined here.

First, heat a pot of water to boiling on the hotplate or stove. Let the class watch as the lid begins jumping up and down. Explain that steam energy lifts the lid. Steam energy can also lift tons of rocks off the top of a mountain when a volcano erupts. Many early-day trains and ships were driven by steam power. And it is steam energy that causes popcorn to pop.

Next, have a child place popcorn in a popper. While the popcorn pops, let the children examine some extra kernels. Tell the children that corn kernels are seeds. Note that they have tough outer coats. Inside the coats, the kernels contain the baby plants and stored food. The food is made of starch and water.

Heat from the popper warms the kernels. As the heat turns the water inside the kernels to steam, the steam pushes against the tough outer coats. The steam gets hotter and pushes harder until the kernels explode. In each explosion, an outer corn kernel coat breaks, the steam escapes into the air, and the starch expands and turns inside out.

While everyone eats the popcorn, mention that popcorn is the only food that turns inside out in this way. Experts tell us that popcorn has existed for at least five-thousand years.

For fun, let the children clap to the following chant:

Popcorn! Popcorn!   We like popcorn
Watch it blow its top.   Right from the pot.
Popcorn! Popcorn!   We like popcorn
Hear the kernels pop.   While it's still hot!

                                        Sarah A. House

 **The Nose Knows**

OCCASION: Christmas
PURPOSE: to explore the sense of smell
MATERIALS: 35-mm film canisters, various things which have scents (see list below), gauze, rubber bands, articles that go with the scented items (optional)